THE AUTOBIOGRAPHY
OF AN ORDINARY WOMAN

Snapshots of a Life

also

A Study of the Aspects of Love

by Ron Roman

 en Press

First published in Great Britain by Pen Press
an Imprint of Indepenpress Publishing Ltd
25 Eastern Place
Brighton
BN2 1GJ

ISBN 978-1-906710-93-4

Printed and bound in the UK

A catalogue record of this book is available from
the British Library

Cover design by Jacqueline Abromeit

Sometimes words flow better with a pen in hand.

Contents

Go for a walk, you'll find something interesting. Are the owners of this car moving house, going on a long holiday or making a comic film? Have a read! It's just the same in my life's story.

PROLOGUE

Ordinary women are the bread and butter, the potatoes and rice, that sustain generation after generation. Behind every genius, inventor, discoverer, are ordinary women preparing the food, making the bed, giving love and comfort. There is infinite variety in these women, even twins have their differences. I make so bold as to share my life with whoever reads this book. I tell the truth, I do not try to be anything but what I really am. In a nutshell, I am a very ordinary middle class wife and mother. Some may agree, some may disagree, with the way I deal with both good and difficult situations.

During a long life, aspects of love have touched me like an outside force coming in when most needed. In this book I liken it to red roses given by a stranger.

For obvious reasons I use a pen name. 'Ron' is my 'baby name' for Veronica.

keeping it warm enough. Dreadful ignorance, I am afraid. My mother asked Mr Longmate to take the rabbit away as it was obviously dying. In front of me, the toddler owner, he picked the rabbit up by its hind legs, and bashed its head violently against the garden wall.

It had an instant death to be sure, but I was petrified with horror and can still recall those awful moments. I also had to recover from the sad scene of my mother drowning the many surplus kittens that regularly populated our garden. A few years later when she did the same with our spaniel's brood, I was devastated. This dog was a pedigree, while on heat she ran off into the Abbey gardens. I'm sure we could have sold those pups, they looked adorable. I can still recall the lovely picture of a mother dog pressing her babies to her teats, sadly, babies to be snatched away, never to be seen again.

I know by personal experience that eggs and chicken flesh have a better texture and taste, when the chicken can forage on waste ground. It is the same with pork. Also, when pigs were fed on the waste food from hotels and restaurants, this now banned 'pig swill' gave the flesh taste and tenderness. I am talking from personal experience. I had an uncle who fed his pigs on the waste food from most of Lincoln's hotels. Of course it was sterilised by boiling, and mixed with standard pig food. The pigs were housed in large sties, not 'free range', I think this is what made their flesh tender as they lazed about, and seemed quite happy. One day my uncle packed up and returned the many items of cutlery thrown into the swill. 'Never do this again,' was the appalled reception, 'we will all get the sack.' I have seen 'free range' pigs in fields as I pass in the car. Certainly they have a little garden as it were, but I am sure that my uncle's pigs, guzzling the swill in their warm sties made the best pork.

In the days of my childhood, working class families had a settled way of life that is missing now. The man had a job for life, his local club, and his allotment. His wife stayed at home looking after the children. Holiday was a trip to the coast by charabanc. This was the life of many of our tenants, so again I speak from personal knowledge. Sometimes an allotment holder would come round selling freshly picked fruit and vegetables. Runner beans, tomatoes and carrots, each had smell and taste, and needed very little cooking. If they brought poultry it was cheap, but you had to gut, clean and pluck it yourself.

I have prepared poultry myself, and 'put a pig away', pies, brawn, sausage, bacon, the lot. It was a nice job on a cold winter's day, and a sizzling fry-up of tasty pieces awaited you when the work was done.

How quiet the roads were until the car arrived. Huge cart horses pulled the dust carts which were all open, shedding fragments of waste around, and pot holes had to be avoided by the wary cyclist. In summer we used to count the men starting to come out in straw hats. 'Foggy straw benger, seggy straw benger,' we yelled. This was child-speak for 'first straw hat, second straw hat.'

It was safe to play on the streets, in the Abbey gardens, the arboretum, and even in the willow fields at the far end of Monk's Rd, which was then a country lane. 'The willows' were a favourite picnic spot. The stream had tadpoles and tiny fish, and nearby, walnut trees where you could gather nuts still in their outer coats, fallen to the ground. The Abbey had a child's playground and a maypole. I always had grazed knees from falling off the swing that I was badly attached to. The large bowling green was at one time looked after by the father of one of my sister's friends. He taught us how to play bowls, and loved to sit us on his knee and bounce us up and down. Today, as I write this, he would be had up for child molesting. It was fun, it was innocent. In the streets we played with whip and top, making chalk designs on the 'window brekkers' that when spun, made a nice pattern. We knew many ball games that did not entail annoying the neighbours, and skipping was quite an art form.

One of the first cars in Lincoln. My father at
the wheel, uncle with pipe, mother (looking
very haughty) and grandmother (with hat!).

Holiday at Skegness with Mother and her sister
(Auntie Lolla) in favourite shelter, backs to wind.
My sister, cousin and self – we girls are wearing
school hats.

The policeman was your friend, your Bobby. One day when I was quite small I went off with my mother's long-handled sweeping brush and swished all along the arboretum railings. Our local policeman came along and took my free hand saying, 'My goodness, you're a long way from home, come, I'll take you back.' And he did.

Another vivid memory I have is cigarette card collecting. Most men smoked, and some women. (My mother gave it a go, using a very long holder.) All packs were sold with excellent cards which could be built up into a set. I used to stand outside my home and accost every man that passed, 'Have you got any cigarette cards?' Invariably they would open their jackets and bring a few out of a top pocket. Can you imagine children being safe doing this now!

What HAS happened! Instead of being a family friend, all a policeman's time is taken up chasing terrorists, muggers, murderers, child molesters, or gangs of teenagers seeking vicious thrills.

My childhood, dating back almost to the oil lamp, was safe and happy, giving me the strong foundation to see me through the following years.

The house we lived in had been built by my grandfather for the family home. It faces the Abbey, and the present owners are doing a really lovely modernisation. It is quite spacious, having three bedrooms, attic, good sized front sitting room, dining room, kitchen, scullery and pantry. Also a bathroom and toilet.

The front garden is small but adequate. My mother put in a show of yellow chrysanthemums, which were always plucked by Labour voters on election day. A good sized back garden goes uphill, where in my day, at the top, was a large wash house with coal-fired boiler (later, gas) and a toilet. It is rumoured that this house is built over a secret tunnel made by the monks to escape to the cathedral when Henry VIII destroyed the monasteries. When I lived there I had various experiences that remain vivid to me today. These experiences were 'out the blue', spontaneous, and very real, certainly not drug induced, nor the hallucinations of a sick mind. Now, at this moment as I try to explain how my life was moulded to make the person that I am today, I must fit them into the jigsaw, for leaving them out, together with others to occur later, would be like trying to solve a crossword without clues.

The first was when I was a baby, just able to pull myself up by the cot railings. The cot was by a wall. Suddenly a bright red lizard-like creature was painted as a living thing on this wall. It oozed evil and terrified me. I screamed and my mother came running. I was not yet able to speak, but I pointed to the wall and screamed. Fortunately my mother realised that the wall had something to do with my terror, and moved the cot to another place. I was far too young to know anything about evil, devils, or that a red lizard is used as a symbol of the devil. It was as if I were being given a book about evil that I could not read, but would come in handy at a later date. For thirty years I dare not face a wall when in bed. I was being told that evil is a real thing, to be feared. Much later my mother kept all her stock of booze in a cupboard in that very place. Evil was trying to get in.

My next experience occurred when I was about eight years old. My sister and I slept in twin beds in the back bedroom. One night I had a never-to-be-forgotten dream, maybe a vision. The room was filled with creamy white angels with folded lengthy wings, and playing harps. They were packed closely together and in between them deliciously smelling rose petals sprayed up and down like a fountain, a fountain of rose petals. In the morning I told my sister, 'Our room was filled with pale women playing harps, they had wings, and a fountain of lovely smelling rose petals sprayed all over.' 'Were they over me too?' she asked. 'Oh yes,' I assured her, and she smiled. Though I was eight, and went to a good school, I had no knowledge of religion, nor had I been to Sunday school, or church service. I had never seen pictures of angels with wings playing harps. I now see this dream as my second 'book' to be read later. I was being told, again in well-known picture form, that there is also a living force of 'good' in our world. An aspect of what, for a better name, we call 'God'.

I was almost twenty when I had a mind-boggling nightmare.

Thinking I was being mature and grown up, I opted for a bedroom apart from my sister, so settled myself in the small bedroom at the back, near the bathroom and toilet. I had not been there long when a nightmare terrified me into going back to my sister in the twin bedroom. (The lovely character that she was, she never said a nasty word about this.) In this nightmare I saw and heard someone trying to get through the window (which opened over the sloping roof of the pantry, thus easy to reach). I screamed blue murder, and again poor mama came running. I can still recall the drumming of my heart. No one was there, evil was trying to get in. Was I being warned? I was tested almost to breaking point in later years, and the 'books' I was being given now were perhaps my salvation.

Some years later my mother was looking after a little boy, the son of tenants called away on business. He had exactly the same nightmare in that room. My mother promptly had the window barred. Again looking back, all this had something to do with the monks of long ago. A force of evil was trying to get a foothold here and vanquish the angel choir of the monks. Maybe this is fanciful thinking, some would think so. But I have lived long enough to see a little 'as through a glass darkly'.

My last and most soul destroying experience was when I was in my mid twenties. The mother we would love to have loved was gradually taking to more and more drink and my heart 'turned over' to watch it, a sort of chill went through me. One night I came in late, and no one was about. The doors were unlocked.

I went to bed. In the morning I was horrified to see my sister was not in her bed. My mother had locked herself in her room and would not answer. In haste I dressed and went to look for my sister. Eventually I found her in her office in the town. She was head of an insurance office. She had a big blanket, and had slept there. She told me she had walked to the office with the blanket over her head, and screaming and crying so that people veered away in alarm. She said she had come home to find our mother in the boozy state we knew too well. Somehow it was the last straw that broke the camel's back. She went upstairs, took all her mother's bottles of drink from the bedroom cupboard, went into the back bedroom which overlooks the garden, and threw them out the window heavily onto the concrete path below. (The next-door neighbour later told us she was terrified at what was going on.) Our mother fled upstairs and locked herself in her bedroom, and in so doing fell heavily against the dressing table, giving herself a black eye. Later, people thought my sister had given her this black eye – well, she had, in a way.

This was the end of our living at home, we rented a house at the other end of town, taking Cuff-links, the mongrel dog, with us. A word or two about Cuff-links. We had taken him when his owner died, his owner being an old sweetheart of my grandmother. They married in their seventies, and had a few years together, my grandmother dying first. Cuff-links was so called because he had a large fluffy head and a large fluffy tail, with a long slender body between. He could safely walk alone, the length of Lincoln, over two railway crossings to get from his home to ours. He never had a lead. He was a dedicated guard dog. When he was with my sister and I, he always put himself on the landing between our two bedrooms at night. Sadly, in the end, he had to be destroyed because he went too far with this guarding and started to attack people.

Just a word or two here about the dangers of obesity. When we left home to live away from our mother, two dear friends helped us and took us in till we found a suitable place to rent. they were sisters, and shockingly fat, did gorgeous cookery, and ate too much. One developed appendicitis and went into hospital. The surgeon had great difficulty in getting to her appendix through all the layers of fat, and was too late to take it out before it burst and the septic fluids killed her. She was greatly mourned.

Very recently I could not resist asking the present owners of the Monk's Rd. house if I could look inside again after all these years. They very kindly let me in, and I was amazed at the transformation. The dark sombre atmosphere was gone, and the best word that comes to mind is 'happy'. Dare I say it! The monks have won hands down. Their 'angels' have driven out the 'lizard' and as they say in the Orange adverts, 'the future's bright'.

On the beach. My mother made those dresses from a curtain!

On the donkeys.

Chapter 2

GROWING UP, SAME SEX FRIENDSHIP, AND MARRIED MEN.

I can remember now the strange feeling that came over me when I suddenly realised life was much more than being a carefree child. I was slow to 'grow up' and quite short-sighted. Until my grandmother remarked to my mother, 'That bairn needs glasses', my schoolwork suffered as I could not read the blackboard, though having a front row desk. I often asked the girl sitting next to me to tell me what was written there. When I at last had the necessary glasses, I could not believe what I saw. 'What a spotty face you've got,' I rudely said to a friend. My schoolwork so improved I gained top marks in most subjects, except maths. Maths was badly taught. The teacher came into the room and wrote on the blackboard a difficult problem. Only a few brains in the class had an inkling as to what it was all about, and this teacher had fun with them working it out, while the rest of us were bored to death and learned nothing. After this debacle I was sent down to a lower division where the teacher was just the opposite, and in the next exams I beat the marks of some of the clever dicks in the first division, who had been given a difficult test. The head was a tiny woman and a very good disciplinarian. To be sent to her for bad behaviour was terrifying. She supported new young teachers when unruly classes took over. There were quite a few real old spinsters. The geography teacher was one. First of all the windows had to be shut, which had been opened by the previous teacher. Then, 'Open your atlas' was the command, and she would ramble on about some holiday she had spent in the place we were looking at. That was the lesson. When, for a change, a sweet little young English teacher arrived, she was adored and brought so many flowers she swamped the staff room, and it had to be stopped. The day always began and ended with prayers, and we had to kneel on the hard wooden floor of the hall. We had a large playing field, and plenty of gymnastic lessons.

Our athletic young gymnastic teacher once called me 'a broken down cab horse' because I was not very good at climbing ropes and 'ribs'. It's funny how one remembers such apt descriptions of oneself. However, armed with my glasses, I got into the hockey team, and in later years played wing in a few games for Lincolnshire. Tennis was my other main game, at which I was a good average. The glass lenses of my glasses were quite dangerous, I once had them break into my eyes, and bits of glass continued to fall out for several days. Fortunately, there was no lasting damage. I have seventeen stitches very neatly done down my right cheek from another fall. Now I am old I have a horror of falling, so am super careful. But my glasses gave me the best of both worlds, both near and distance were good. Recently I had cataract treatment on both eyes and the brilliance of colours suddenly revealed dazzled me. But for near, short sight, I now have to use magnifying lenses. In the days of wearing glasses I could take them off to see clearly the tiniest of writing. Things have sort of reversed. It is great to do without glasses – out in the rain, swimming, reading signposts, many things without the need of glasses are so much improved.

The wonderful world of invention has done so much for me – without my two hip replacements I would be in a wheelchair, without excellent false teeth eating would be a nightmare, without my mobility scooter I would be confined to the house, without various pills I would probably die of a stroke – I could go on! My first hip operation was done by Professor Sir John Charnley himself. It lasted some thirty years before needing attention, even then not complete replacement. He was very particular, operating under a complete plastic 'tent' rendered totally sterile. He came to take the stitches out himself, not leaving it to a nurse. So you met this small man with the boyish face and he smiled and sort of stroked your wound as if giving it healing. One brief meeting but he is a photo in my mind forever. He died young, so my future operations were done by a surgeon who had trained under him, and it gave me great comfort to know this. I was not disappointed. All this was at King Edward VII hospital near Midhurst. Now closed! Can you believe it!

If you will forgive me I am going to jump right forward from my school days to the very present. It is a lovely sunny day so I went out on my mobility scooter to park on the grassy verge along Marine Parade East. The verge slopes down to the pebble beach, and the Solent water that separates Hampshire from the Isle of Wight. The water dazzled with golden ripples, Osborne House peeped at me through a gap in the trees, small sailing boats sailed forth by the shores of the Isle of Wight, large cargo vessels made for Southampton docks, a flock of starlings amused themselves weaving swirling patterns in the air, noisy helicopters buzzed overhead, and people, old and young lay about or slowly paraded past me absorbing as much sun as possible. I slowly munched through a bag of fruit I had taken with me, and thought happily, as the song goes, 'what a wonderful world'. Why on earth do terrorists exist? Why is there so much evil? This lovely world should make us all happy! If only every child born could be given a kick-start, given the chance to make the best of the circumstances that his particular life had put him into. Oh dear, this 'if only'!

My next thoughts were, 'I wonder how much longer I have got, what will I die of? What will death of the body bring me to?' As I sat pondering, a little rhyme came into my head that I would like to leave with my family when I do depart from this world. Here it is.

AT MY DEPARTING
Bathe me with your love,
Dear Jesus,
Wash my sins away,
Let your grace and truth

Come in,
May my life with you begin,
And forever stay.

I am not a regular church goer, though I was christened, and confirmed into the Church of England. People I have met, and experiences I have had, have brought Christianity into my life. Nothing so dramatic as St. Paul's conversion, but equally convincing.

A long life has taught me this truth, we must build on our past, not hover in it, not yearn for it, but swallow its lessons through birth, childhood, teens, middle age, old age, to death. Shakespeare is so right when he says, 'There is a destiny that shapes our ends, rough hew them though we may'. What I am today is the result of how I have handled my destiny, the destiny I cannot escape from. How I have handled the periods of despair, sorrow and pain, as well as the times of health and happiness. As I have said, my childhood gave me a lot, a firm foundation on which to build. It saw me through both mental and physical upsets, and brought me to an old age that my doctor recently called, 'switched on'. Being 'middle class' I began with certain advantages. I did not get rickets through lack of vitamins as did some poor children who played in the Abbey with me. Nor did I have to say, 'Please give me your apple core when you have finished.' My personal belief is that we are born with certain advantages won for us by our ancestors. Some have to pay for the evil perpetrated by their ancestors. When I conquered a near nervous breakdown my first thoughts were, 'thank goodness my children will not have to go through this, I have conquered it'!

Perhaps many will think me fanciful, but experiences in my life have made me come to the conclusion that individuals are part of a large spiritual family, both living and dead, and family members can help or hinder. We may be born into Hitler's family, we may be born into that of our Queen. Whoever we are we must live, as the hymn says, 'through all the changing scenes of life, in trouble and in joy'.

One life – so much to be seen. The peacock
seems to be saying it all – 'Just look'.

My son and I leave the car to gaze at the
jacaranda trees in Pretoria, South Africa.

Twice a day I had a long walk uphill to school, for I came home to midday meal, called 'dinner'. With friends I went up through the arboretum in sun, rain and snow, often with a heavy satchel of books. My school had good discipline, no racial tensions, and a respect for the Church of England, the government, and those elected to authority.

Quite recently I was watching the panorama of people on the beach. A large group of Muslims came by. They were good-looking, tall and slim, the women putting our obese matrons, and the men our pot-bellied beer drinkers, to shame. How did I know they were Muslims? The women wore pretty dresses that covered them from head to foot, blocking out all the vitamin D given by the sun. The men wore turbans, and were dressed in town clothes, in sharp variance to the half-naked crowd of English. They sat on the pebbles right in front of a family and totally blocked the view of the sea! I am not going to pass any judgement, but I do think that people who choose to live in our country, and are accepted by us, should try to conform to our way of life.

I took a long time to grow up. Many young girls were married, even grandmothers, long before any sex instinct roused me. My first steady friend was a woman some fourteen years my senior. There was nothing lesbian in this friendship, but she gave me the deepest love I have ever known. We liked the same things, country walks, exploring old village churches, paddling in every pond or stream we passed, and reading good books. We had three glorious weeks in Switzerland, and I often went to her home in Northern Ireland. She was very religious, and went on retreats every year. One day we were sat together on a seat in the arboretum facing a beautiful circular bed of begonias. Lucy, that was her name, (she is now dead) had her hands in her pockets. In a moment of friendliness I put my hand over hers in the pocket near to me. As I did so it seemed that electric lights switched on in every flower, outdoing the sun. They slowly faded back to normal. It was Lucy's love for me that caused this vision. I never told her. 'Touch me, and you'll know what happiness is' goes the Andrew Lloyd Webber song. One description of 'happiness' could be 'spiritual love'.

I now realise the value of the years spent as Lucy's friend. Not for me school sex behind the bike shed, motherhood in my teens, and a Coronation Street life to follow.

The Northern Ireland I knew all those years ago was very warm in heart and very wet in body. Once I was there for the whole of July, and it rained every day. We went for walks passing cattle huddled into corners with their backs towards the rain, and trees bent over by the prevailing wind. The family dog sniffed among the hedgerows which threw out the pungent smell of meadowsweet. Banks of fuchsia dropped a profusion of little red flowers like the blood drops of the future men of the 'troubles'. The beach was called 'the strand'. The huge breakers made swimming dangerous, but there was a handy large rock pool where Lucy could dive in from a high rock. My eyesight without my glasses was so poor, diving frightened me as I could not see what I was diving into. Laser treatment and contact lenses were things I had never heard of.

Sometimes we would walk up to 'Wee Jinny' and buy her griddle pancakes. They tasted delicious because they were made of local ground flour, and the griddle greased with pure pig lard. Wee Jinny certainly was not wee, she fitted into her small thatched cottage like a large pumpkin in a box. If only this gorgeous lard could be bought now! The modern pressed wax that passes for lard in the supermarkets does not make the delicious pastry I made for my children. They all remember it and say, 'Mum, make some of those lovely mince pies, an apple tart, or a bramble pie.' My answer is, 'I cannot, I cannot get the right fat, mixtures of butter and other available fats are just not the same.' Maybe in some places the unprocessed pure pig lard is still available, but not where I live.

From a local farmer we bought fresh churned butter, creamy milk produced that morning, and eggs that would make today's most expensive free range seem watery and tasteless. Bread was made at home, one big baking day making enough for the week. The local speciality was 'balm bract' (if I have spelt it right) a very tasty mixed wholemeal.

Potatoes, another staple food, were grown at home, and dug up as required. They were usually cleaned, boiled in their skins, and given to you on a side plate by your meal. You peeled them yourself. They are exceedingly fluffy and tasty, and with a dab of butter or cheese make a meal in themselves. Isa, Lucy's sister was the cook, her thin arms wielding the heavy, sooty pans from kitchen table to fire and back in a manner only practice had made perfect. These potatoes when mashed and added to the juices of a boiled ham made a soup to dream of. Boiled leg of Irish pork was taken from the pot, drained, and the fat on top pricked and salted. It was then put into a very hot oven until it had a crown of gold on top. In those years when the potato crop failed due to adverse weather conditions, and the poor, who had little else to live on, starved, or left their homeland in droves, the British Isles should have come to their help. James Galway and Phil Coulter have made a lovely cd called *Winter's Crossing* all about this tragedy. We never seem to know how to deal with Ireland. 'The troubles' would never have come about if we had let north and south join up, and then invited united Ireland to become a part of the United Kingdom. I am no politician. Some would find many reasons why this could not be done.

Now, I am ashamed to tell you I ditched Lucy quite suddenly. Something seemed to tell me to move on. A woman partner was not my destiny. Though there was nothing lesbian in our relationship, I know she thought the very same as my sister, who years later when I married said, 'I'm losing my life partner.'

For fifteen years I was a teacher of what was then called domestic science, having done well in the higher certificate, the final leaving exam of High School. In my youth I had a 'picture memory' that made exams easy for I 'saw' in my mind the page of a book or a whole poem. I was not exactly a 'born' teacher, but I got along with a few ups and downs. I started off in a nice village school, and should have stayed there for the pupils were gentle country kids, well brought up. I moved to be back again in Lincoln, living with my mother and sister. The school I moved to was a different kettle of fish. It was part of a large new estate built to accommodate families evacuated from barges in Brayford water, a large stretch of water in central Lincoln. The children were graded into classes A, B, and C, according to intelligence. The C children were tricky to handle, but fortunately for me, loved simple cookery and did not mind the cleaning up, indeed, liked it much better than lessons, so much so I could ask their form mistress to send a few along to clean up the awful messes left by the As and Bs. It was a mixed school with boys and girls, and male and female staff. The cookery room was in a separate block with the woodwork and science rooms. During 'break' the children were all given little glass bottles of milk, and they liked to come into the cookery room to make cocoa. The woodwork and science teachers also joined me with their staffroom tea. They often bought the children's cakes, eyeing them and the children. 'Ah well,' the science teacher remarked, 'The oven is a good sterilizer.'

I always had the C children making soups and stews to show them how to make a cheap meal. One mother came in regularly to buy some, often trading in clothes coupons as she had no money. The second world war was in full swing. Coupons for clothes, ration books for food. I got used to the powdered egg, the absence of bananas and chocolate, horse meat in the butcher's, and eels being sold as worth a try. I was tempted by the clothes coupons, and sinfully took them.

The woodwork teacher became a friend, and he and his wife taught my sister and I to play contract bridge, which amused us for hours. Television was still in the future, and we were all used to amusing ourselves without the plethora of gadgets that surround us today. My sister and I were now living in a flat surrounded by airmen and their wives and children. They called us 'the girls', and played contract bridge with us many evenings, or left their children with us when they had a night out. The woodwork teacher and his wife were some fifteen years older than my sister and I, but this never mattered. They had no children, the wife being one of those big mannish women who are barren, and I believe had only married to gain marital status. They owned a large farm in Lincolnshire which was rented out, and partly looked after by the tenant. He bought the farm with money that had been saved for a world cruise on retirement. We never heard the end of this, poor, unhappy wife had lost her cruise!

I am going to call this man Tom, not use his real name. There was a cottage on the farm, slightly improved by bringing in mains water. I expect it has been modernised. In my day it had no bathroom, and the toilet was a covered hole in an outside shed some distance away. It has two rooms downstairs and two rooms upstairs, and a north facing, low built scullery which acted as refrigerator quite well. Off the living room there is a kitchen sink, and space for cooking. The lighting was by oil lamp, and the cooking on a small black range in the living room, the fire being the only source of heating. With the fire stoked up, the oven could roast a chicken to perfection. A hook for the kettle ensured you had hot water. By the sink an oil stove supplemented the cooking facilities. No gas, no electricity, no mod cons! I had many a happy weekend there. The garden had a very fruitful apple tree, and several gooseberry bushes. The soil is fertile, and I merrily grew huge radishes, beautiful sweet peas, and threw in every pretty packet of seeds found in the garden centres.

A local riding school used to rest its horses in one of the farm fields, and I was allowed to ride them. They were totally safe, and I hacked around without jumping any five-bar gates, because to tell the truth, I dare not.

Gradually Tom began to rely on me for a bit of comfort. He was not passionate or highly sexed, but his wife gave him nothing. His wife turned a blind eye, we all remained friendly, and she maintained her status as a married woman.

When I was of marriageable age young men were being killed in their thousands in World War II. Married, older men, had a field day. After fifteen years of teaching I had had enough, and retired on a quarter pension. In order to rest I took a job as storekeeper in a small local hospital. I was still living with my sister, and still friendly with Tom, but a young married man who was my boss came after me all guns firing.

He was very tempting as he was so calm and restful to be with, his soft soothing voice was just what I needed in my present nervy state. He had a nice home and one little daughter. Many times he said, 'come to the pictures with me', and I had visions of the back row! I am sure I could have been very happy with him, but absolutely could not build my happiness on the tears of another woman. I told him so, and he knew I meant it. Finally he applied to be moved to another hospital far up North and we parted without touch or kiss, but I will always remember him and his oh so soothing voice.

It was at this hospital that I met my husband. The stores were brought in by lorry from a large hospital some distance away, of which the one I worked in was a branch. The regular driver became ill, and the man who was to become my husband was given the job.

Chapter 3

MARRIAGE, CHILDREN, A HOTEL, AND THE UKRAINE.

The man to be my husband, along with a large group of fellow Ukrainians captured by the Nazis during the war, was at last, after three years, allowed to leave the holding camps in Italy. They had to have stringent health checks before leaving. Not many returned to the Ukraine, because the Communists were still in power. Those who did return were often never heard of again. The war was over, and my future husband, Walter, along with a group of friends, elected to come to England, rather than Canada, another favourite choice. In the holding camps they had learned some English, and had instruction in various crafts. Whilst there they had built themselves a beautiful chapel from the stones, shells and debris around them, and made their bedding with the tall, dry grasses around their tents and sheds. In the end there was no grass left. Their average age was twenty. They arrived in England in just the clothes they wore, and a motley collection of carefully saved family photos. The group I eventually got to know were put on Lincolnshire farms, housed and fed in large hostels, given a small wage, and had to work hard on the land. As time passed, Walter earned extra money by hair cutting, doing overtime driving tractors, or repairing things around the farm. In his own country he was training to be a gunsmith and tool maker. Eventually, he, and one or two of his friends got jobs in a large psychiatric hospital up on Bracebridge Heath on the outskirts of Lincoln. Walter rose to a good job in the stores, in spite of his rather dodgy English. One of his friends became head chef, and others trusted carers. (This hospital was recently dismantled and a large new housing estate and pub now take its place.)

Let's keep bees…

…like Grandad

The Ukrainians are far from lazy. Those that eventually rented or bought small houses in Lincoln kept them brightly painted, with pretty gardens in the smallest of places. In fact you could pick these out and say, 'I bet a Ukrainian lives there!' They had a club room in Lincoln where cigarettes and booze were king and queen. Here they drowned their sorrows, trying to forget all they had lost, family, girlfriends, the food of their homeland, the language that was native and natural. Walter's best friend was in training to be a priest, now he worked in a noisy drop stamping factory.

Getting into their thirties these Ukrainian men were looking round to find wives. They tried the dance halls with some success. Lincoln girls had lost their men in the war, and some, like myself, were heading towards spinsterhood. Walter was fairly short for a man, stocky, muscular and strong. Cossack blood swirled in his veins. One day when he brought in the stores, and during our small talk, he said, 'There's only one thing worthwhile – a home and a family.' And as he said it he filled the little room with a force of love I could feel, as one could feel a cloudy mist. This was not directed particularly at me. There is a Ukrainian saying, 'My trousers are not long enough' meaning, 'I am not good enough for you'. I knew he thought this about me, that I would not consider him as a possible partner.

However he was wrong. 'Good heavens,' I thought, 'that's just what I want.' And in that instant, I knew I would marry him. In a way, we kind of made a bargain, 'we will give each other a home and a family'. Indeed we kept that bargain through many ups and downs, for many years, until he died, eight years ago.

Our first home was a semi-detached in a pretty village, close to Lincoln. Walter could cycle to his work in the hospital. It had a large garden, and we grew all our own fruit and vegetables, also having our own hens and a beehive. We backed onto a big orchard, and the owners were so thankful for our bees they gave us a great deal of luscious fruit. There was also a greenhouse for tomatoes, and a splendid bed of asparagus.

Before I go any further, I must say a word or two about our wedding. 'Tell your mother you are getting married,' Walter said. 'I cannot,' I replied, 'I have not seen or spoken to her in years.' 'Never mind,' Walter said, 'Do it,' so I did, on a scrappy bit of postcard. She did come to the church, and also to the reception which we held in our future home. Walter had played a trump card, he had united a family that had been split for many years. When my sister and I left our mother she almost gave up drinking in terror at what she had done, and took in lodgers who saw the best side of her, and thought highly of her, never knowing she had two estranged daughters, until gossiping tenants told her. At the time of my wedding she was tired and getting old. My sister, also at the wedding, and now living alone, and being the caring person she was, and, too, ignoring the traumatic past, offered her mother two choices – a little bungalow, or, to come and live with her. My mother sensibly chose to live with my sister, did her wonderful cooking, and enjoyed car rides in the little Ford Prefect my sister bought. Twice she looked after me when my first two children were born. I still marvel at Walter's 'good deed'. It gave my sister company when I left, it gave our mother a safe and happy old age, and all of us a sort of 'forget the past, it's over'. Eventually she died of cancer of the throat. My sister nursed her to her death, having to feed her through a tube into her stomach, all the while still doing a full-time office job. May I say here that I do not wish to be kept alive when my quality of life is zero.

My sister was then alone again. She took various 'old dears' on car rides, ran the insurance office, and often treated my children to a day out. They called her 'Aunty Barb' (Barbara), behaved well and loved her.

Some couples spend a fortune on their wedding, Walter and I had a 'do-it-yourself' one. Walter prepared the house for the reception. It had been unsold for some time and needed repairing and cleaning in all rooms. Neighbours were beginning to moan about the spreading of weed seeds from the garden. I made everything for the table from cheese straws to wedding cake. Two lovely begonias decorated the table. We had no honeymoon, I spent the time dealing with the pile of laundry Walter brought with him! This well-built semi with three bedrooms, kitchen, living room and dining room, large south-facing garden, garage, greenhouse, water softener, and large front garden, cost £1,800.

A small shop or two, a doctor, and a good infant school were not far away. Creamy, unpasteurised milk from tuberculin tested cows was delivered daily. The butcher brought chicken, boiling fowl, and meat from a slaughter house where he personally chose the best on offer. I wish I could get boiling fowl now, they make a delicious meal when stewed with cubes of root vegetables. Perhaps, though, the modern boiling fowl, like the modern brisket would not be so tasty and tender as of old. For a short while Sainsburys did sell quite a good boiling fowl imported from France. Minced, it made a good weaning food, far better than any tinned food. Although I did all the baking, cakes one week, pastry the next, I was often tempted by the delicious jam and cream sponge cakes brought round by a large Lincoln firm. This firm also sells its own Lincolnshire sausage, which you cannot beat. It is light, with just the right amount of sage. It can be bought today. My children were all weaned, after breast feeding, on the unpasteurised milk from tuberculin tested cows, and on exactly what Walter and I were eating, minced up. I never bought a tin of baby food, and my children only had the usual childish illnesses – measles, mumps and chickenpox, which they all caught when they started school. The fact that many mothers have to go out to work to bring enough money into the home, causing children to be left alone or with babysitters, is perhaps at the root of many of today's problems. The mother comes home tired, so relies on the quick fix, the tinned and shop-prepared food. These foods are often too sugary, salty or fatty. A bad diet in infancy can lead to future ill health, obesity, or even anti-social behaviour. All through this autobiography I am attempting to trace the various aspects of love that have touched me. I looked up the word, 'love', in my crossword dictionary, but got no help. Like the word, 'grace', it is a little word that is like a spyhole looking onto a vast landscape. So far I have tried to describe the childhood dream of angels, the lights in the flowers when I held Lucy's hand, Walter's misty cloud of love, all absolutely true experiences, flowers in the great bouquet of love.

I am totally convinced that world peace can never be brought about by war, nor even negotiation, and that until every child born is conceived with love, born with love and nurtured with love, strife will always batter our world.

My three children were all born at home, with the help of the district midwife and doctor. When my husband rang up in the night to summon the midwife to help me with my first child a nurse turned up different from the one I had been seeing. She was good, and oiled and massaged me to ease the birth. Later the nurse I was used to turned up, then over my prostrate body they had a real slanging match! 'Why did you go away when you knew your patient was about due?' shouted the first nurse, 'this is my rest day.' 'I had to,' stated the other, 'my son got married.' 'Blow that,' spat out the first nurse, 'your duty lies here.' Eventually she left in a huff, and the second nurse, the one I knew, took over. She was an absolutely top-class midwife, and never lost a baby. You would never think it to look at her. She was very small, and always looked as if she had dressed in a hurry. She had a twin sister, and they both went to Africa to nurse. There she met and married a missionary, had three children who towered over her, joined 'Lepra' to nurse in a leper colony, and did not turn a hair at amputating a man's leg with an axe! Her husband died young, and left her to bring up their family on her own, back home in England.

The morning came and I was still in labour. As I was nearly forty, and this my first baby, she summoned the doctor, who wisely told me to ignore the 'pushes' and rest. This I did for a while, when suddenly my daughter, who jolly well has a mind of her own, decided to get some air, and thrust her head out so forcefully I let out a terrific scream. The doctor slapped my face, thinking I was going into hysterics. As my daughter came into the world a most powerful love overwhelmed me, so much so, I kissed the doctor who was bending over me. She looked very surprised, and apologised for slapping me earlier. This great flood of love happened every time I gave birth, but I refrained from kissing, again as it took a bit of explaining. I did not expect, did not seek, did not pray for this love, it came as a gift, as one might be given a red rose by a complete stranger. In my day it certainly was not common for husbands to be present at their wife's side as she gave birth. I know my husband was worried about it all, and I could hear him in the bathroom next door, where he had strategically placed himself as close as possible.

This midwife became a lifelong friend, I always called her, 'Nursie'. My two other children are boys. The first was an easy birth, the second, one of Nursie's triumphs. She turned him over, without giving me any pain, so that his head and not his feet came first, then straddled over me helping with the pushes in just the right places. When he emerged I do not know which of us was the hottest, we were both panting and sweating. Today I would be rushed off to hospital for a Caesarian. Luckily for me I had never heard of cot death, nor that older mothers could have mentally retarded children. I had no false fears, no pre-birth scans, and many happy years were ahead of me.

The day arrived when we came to the end of my savings, and Walter's earnings were not enough to support our growing family. We decided to try our luck with a small bed and breakfast hotel in Bournemouth. The children had the chance of better schooling, and the seaside was a healthy environment. The hotel was a little goldmine, and we soon had our mortgage paid off. But there was a price to pay.

The roof leaked in several places, and Walter had to place buckets to collect water before it got to the bedrooms. Before we bought we only had one view inside, and the owner cunningly said he had no ladder for us to go up and look at the roof. We were innocents abroad, and he knew it (he was an Italian Jew). Later on we became convinced he had swapped good furniture and bedding, for charity shop seconds. We did have one good laugh over the roof debacle. One night the rain did drip through onto a foreign student, and he came down to thank us for sprinkling him with the pink holy water on just the right day and at just the right time.

The boiler, which was in our private sitting/bed room, constantly broke down, and Walter spent whole nights fixing it so that our guests had hot water in the morning. We had no spare cash to pay for all the work that needed doing.

The fact that we prospered was mainly due to Walter. I looked after the business side, and did the cooking, but without Walter's great handyman's skills the hotel would not have made the money it did. What I tell you now may make your hair stand on end! There was one bathroom for all the guests, and wash basins in every bedroom. In summer Walter converted this one bathroom into a single bedroom, by skilfully converting the bath into a bed! Can you imagine this being possible now? He did this so well no visitor ever complained, indeed it was a popular room, being near the toilet, and having a window getting the morning sun. One man even gave us a ten pound tip, which was a lot in those days. We shared our own bathroom with the guests, so they came through our own sitting room to reach it. Some foreign students had lovely shy smiles as they did so. It was a different world! Guests were happy without the en suite, without the tea and coffee making equipment, without a television. I brought round the cups of tea in the morning, and that was their wake-up call.

There were two well equipped chalets in the garden, and our own caravan. We let them all, though it was against the law. The people who rented them were happy-go-lucky trippers, who liked the outside life. We left our doors open so that they could use our toilet and bathroom, it being perfectly safe then to do so. In the morning they lined up at the back door to fetch their breakfasts.

As soon as we put up a vacancy notice, cars swarmed into our car park. French boys got into trouble because they parked on the pavement as they were used to at home. Our speciality was a really good breakfast, and this brought people back again and again. They would even sleep in the lounge, if we would make the sofa up into a bed. Walter carried large boxes of fresh tomatoes from a local shop, we never used tinned. The eggs were very fresh, and the men were given two which highly pleased them!

In winter Walter converted the largest rooms into bed-sits. We became friendly with the people who rented them, often enjoying Christmas drinks together. There was no 'squatting' and no other trouble. We did have a visit from the police. If we had converted all the rooms it would have been illegal. A brother and sister wanted to stay with us till they died, saying they would leave us all their money. We did not feel we could cope with this, but remained friendly when they moved into a large flat near Bournemouth gardens. Our hotel was not detached, it was attached to a private house owned by two dear old ladies. Our plan was to buy this house when they sold.

Looking back from a distance of many years, I can see now how I was improved and helped by those three doses of supreme love that were given to me at the birth of my children.

In my horse riding, tennis and hockey days I used to say 'Flipping kids, who wants them'. And when teaching I looked evilly at a tin of rat poison with the picture of a particularly troublesome child in my head. A tremendous dose of parental love had made its home in me.

It is time now to say a word or two about Walter. When he was born his country was ruled by Poland, and not treated very well. Then came the Communists, and things got even worse. His parents owned acres of pine forest, and kept very many beehives in order to make a pine honey that had medicinal qualities. A fierce dog ran round and round the field that contained the beehives, chained to a rail on the surrounding fence. Their farm was in Zolochev, a climate healthy area near the Carpathian mountains. In summer they took in people needing this healthy air. There was also a large orchard, vegetable garden, poultry, a working horse, and a cow or two. When the Communists came everything was confiscated, leaving Walter's parents with a little of their orchard, a few hens, and one cow and calf. The hens were calculated to lay a certain amount of eggs which had to be handed in.

If you did not join the Communist party, you could not go into higher education, travel outside your district, nor advance yourself in any way. Some of Walter's relatives were carted off to Siberia and never heard of again, he even saw his special girl friend go this way. Walter, with friends, went underground to plan revenge tricks. One day he was captured and made to dig his own grave with a Russian standing over him pointing a gun. He had nearly finished when a shot rang out, and he fell into his grave thinking a bullet had struck him. But, no, a friend stalking by had spotted what was going on, and shot the Russian. Walter told me he ran home white-faced and trembled violently for two weeks.

Next the Nazis came in and fooled some Ukrainians into joining them by saying they would oust the Russians. They actually forced other Ukrainians into their army, Walter being one. These Ukrainians were really prisoners ordered to fight, and thankfully, at the end of the war, the English realised this, and gave many a home.

On his shoulders were marks where bullets had grazed, but most of all was the damage done to him as a person. He told me he trusted no one, and for years depended on heavy smoking. He had regular dreadful screaming attacks, which at first frightened me to death. They were never directed against me, it was a kind of self hate, revulsion at what had become of him. Never once did he threaten me or the children, he would rush upstairs and lie on the bed, screaming his heart out. I think the modern term is 'post war stress syndrome'. Eventually, I would take up a cup of tea, and he would gradually calm down. The English worship of the cup of tea used to amuse him, but he got quite converted. 'I am a tree half chopped down,' he would say. He envied his children their education, the education he had been denied, their fluent English (a language he found hard to master for it is 'Roman', not 'Cyrillic'), and perhaps most of all, their happy freedom.

He tried to get work in the trade he knew, but did not have the English qualifications, so was turned away.

I called him the unhappy immigrant. England had given him a home, wife, children, work, car, holidays, but somehow nothing could wash him clean. It is sometimes possible to mend a broken body, sometimes possible to revive a broken spirit. How I wish I could have done more for Walter.

Most of his friends were quite the reverse, and settled in like adopted puppies. He could drink a bottle of whiskey and not turn a hair. He bemoaned the fact that he could not get drunk and forget everything! He once drove me home perfectly safely after a party where he had drunk enough to damage his liver. When he gave up smoking his moods got worse. I really think that in his case it would have been better for him to reduce rather than give up entirely. For all our marriage he was hard working and faithful. His presence was enough to discipline the children, and corporal punishment, which was not banned at the time, was never used. My children were the last generation to be let free safely, eat unprocessed food, and amuse themselves without all the modern gadgetry. The unmanageable children now depicted on television, the gangs of dope-taking, knife-wielding youths, the pregnant schoolgirls, the shops selling cheap booze, have all matured in my lifetime. When not at school my children all helped in the hotel, my daughter as waitress, my two sons as bedroom tidiers. They had a lot of freedom because we were too busy to fuss over them.

When the Ukraine gained its freedom from Communism, we were at last free to visit Walter's family. We took over money and many presents. Walter's niece, Helena, put us up. She had her mother, Walter's sister living with her. It was the family home Walter knew. The house obtained its water from a pump in the garden. The oven was heated by bottled gas. The only toilet was made from a hole in the ground at some distance from the house. There was electric light and television. A large enclosed stove heated the house in winter. There was no 'upstairs'. The welcome was amazing, it was as if we were thrown into a bath of love! For years they had thought Walter dead, his name was on the village memorial, and here he was alive and well, with wife and three children they hoped to see next visit. New modern-style houses were being put up. This took time as money could not be borrowed from banks, nor any form of mortgage be obtained. So, with your first available money you bought the land, later put in foundations, then year by year the whole house came into being, often on land without roads or services, until these were added later. Some of Walter's relations were building on land that was the garden of their present home.

It was obvious that Walter's family would have done better if they had been allowed higher education. Helena especially stood out.

Walter's parents with his sister.
Walter's photo is on the wall – they
believed he was killed in the war.

Family party with home-made vodka.
'Carpet' on the wall. Women in 'head scarf'.

Old ladies of the village. They always covered their hair.

New houses near Zolochev.

On our visits Walter played the Ukrainian folk songs on his mouth organ, and enjoyed true Ukrainian food, and chatted with his sister in his own language. I asked him if he would like to spend half the year in the Ukraine and half in England. He would not do this, he had got used to the safety and comfort of England.

Walter had the sort of death I would like. He had just turned eighty. He walked in from the garden and sat in his usual chair opening the *Echo*, our local paper. I said, 'I'll just go in the other room to see if we have an email from Stan,' the son then in Saudi Arabia. When I came back I thought he had fallen asleep. I could not wake him and in a panic, dialled 999. An ambulance and neighbours all arrived quickly. We were then in our retirement home in Poole. It was like a scene often depicted in television dramas. Mouth-to-mouth resuscitation and many electric shocks failed to start his heart beating, he was dead, caused by a clot. He had suffered from arthritis, and one hip replacement, otherwise was a healthy person. He had given me a lot, kept his side of the bargain, and I shall always feel that even through the bad days there ran a thread of gold.

His religion was Celtic Orthodox, and the funeral people I employed found me just the right priest to bless him on his way. This priest came to see me, tall, with beard, dressed in full regalia, and leaning on two large crutches. He took one loose from under his arm and it looked as if he were holding a shepherd's staff, resembling a biblical figure. He came in and we discussed the cremation and general burial arrangements. He blessed us all, 'Through the ages of ages'. I chose the hymn, 'Fight the good fight' because it has great wording, 'fight the good fight', 'lay hold on life', 'run the straight race', 'faint not nor fear'. From his first smile at the door I knew immediately this priest to be totally sincere, yes, totally. It is a privilege to know such a person. I asked him not only to 'look after' Walter, but my whole family, and he does.

Chapter 4

HOLIDAY FLATS, HEALERS, CURES.

Our four years in the Bournemouth hotel came to a sudden and dramatic end when we found out we were on a road scheme, and to be demolished for improvements to the railway. Our Lincoln solicitor had badly let us down as he should have found this out and warned us. (A word of advice here, always employ a local solicitor.) Have you ever tried to get a solicitor to sue a solicitor? I just about came to a nervous breakdown, eventually extracting £1,000. This solicitor belonged to a firm used by my family for many years. It had been given the job of checking my mother's handling of the rents when my father died, because the money derived was willed to other members of the family and to my sister and I, not my mother. This was my grandfather's way of keeping the money in the blood line. My mother had to keep books showing money collected, and all expenditures. Here again, the solicitor failed. When my sister and I reached twenty-one the whole business should have been handed over to us. It was not. Out of the blue one day we received a letter advising us to sue our mother. Though we were then estranged from her, we could not do such a vile thing. She wrote a letter of thanks, but we felt sad, not happy. Of course, handing over meant she lost a steady income. She took in lodgers.

The council gave us less money than we would have got from a private sale. We began to look around, and to add insult to injury, when we were about to put a deposit on a place we liked, this same council pushed in to make a children's home. Walter went round on his bike, and spotted some holiday flats near the sea in Boscombe. They were owned by a business man who could not knock a strait nail in, and was tired of the expense of employing labour. He soon had Walter putting a few things right, became friends, and secured us a loan from his bank, when our bank refused. Our bank had a new manager, he regretted this and tried to win me back.

Though these holiday flats made money, they were very hard work for Walter. They had never been modernised, and we could not afford the expense. There was no central heating. Gas fires on meter were in all main rooms, and needed constant attention. The plumbing was old, toilets, wash basins, baths, and taps, kept a tool bag constantly in Walter's hand. Gas ovens had an old-fashioned lighting system that really was a nightmare.

We were near the sea, our prices reasonable, always there in emergencies, clean and friendly, thus keeping a steady flow of regulars.

It was coming to the days of the squatter, and we sometimes had trouble making 'winter' tenants leave when the time came for the summer visitors. Students were regular winter tenants, and many left awful messes and, until Walter adjusted the ground floor windows to only open a little way, smuggled friends in to sleep. People on social security came in with bottles of drink, passing Walter perhaps cleaning the stairs. 'Still at it!' they would remark.

I enjoyed a lot of swimming, and tending the small garden in front of our 'Monster' as we called the flats.

Our daughter was married from here, and our eldest son bought his own house. It was a very busy time, full of incidents. Also, for me, it was a time to savour totally new experiences, that would help and guide me through the coming years.

When we lost our hotel and moved to the holiday flats, the nervous tension brought about by my mother was still lurking in the background. It came forward in a rush over all the trauma involved in dealing with the Lincoln solicitor. I knew I needed some help, and it came in a most unexpected way. I went for a three-week rest in a small hospital that looked after people with nervous illnesses such as eating disorders and breakdowns. There was a young doctor whose permission you had to get if you wanted to go outside for a walk. I had made a friend, and I went in to see if we could have a half hour outside.

He was sat at his desk with his hands folded together on it. He looked at me, smiling, but saying nothing. In an impulse I cannot explain I put a hand gently over his folded hands, and stood wordless. He bent his head, not looking at me, saying nothing, and patiently waiting for me to move away. No words, no drugs, silence, and healing was given and accepted. This, my first experience of healing, was the beginning of my final release from the misery of 'nerves' that had plagued me for years. I was able to gradually take less and less 'dope' until I was completely free, and what a blessing. It is so much better to master yourself without the use of drugs, the result is far more satisfying in every way.

Now I come to an extraordinary chapter in my life, that I find very difficult to write about, because it involves spiritualism and healing, two experiences that, unless you are deeply involved in them, do not seem credible. Also, we have the false prophet, the fake healer, the pretend spiritualist, who dreadfully damages the reputation of genuine people.

I will do my best to tell you what actually happened to me. I was not looking for it, I did not expect it, it came to me as winning the 'Pools' might happen for a prisoner.

Though I was now entirely free from needing any drugs or dope to keep a healthy mind, I was not exactly 'on top of the world'. I was like a good bulb needing soil, water and air to grow. One sunny morning I was sat in the small garden in front of the holiday flats. A lady came up to me and said, 'Your mother has been knocking on our window all night, saying we must tell you to go to a healer.' She was a summer visitor, I had met only once as she paid her deposit. My mother had been dead for some years. Seeking help in a Spiritualist church was not a thing I had ever envisaged, but to be thus accosted intrigued me, and I decided to investigate. How had this complete stranger heard and seen my dead mother? How did she so confidently find me? How did she know it was spiritual healing I needed, not physical, though I had both hips waiting replacement?

I went to the main Spiritualist Church in Bournemouth, and after talking with the lady in charge, allocated a healer.

The healer sent to me was a man some fourteen years older than myself, homely and easy to befriend. He sat behind me and placed his hands lightly on my shoulders. His hands were cool, but a cosy warmth spread through my body, and when I walked home along the promenade I felt as if I had just awoken from a refreshing night's sleep. From being a sceptic, I was becoming a convert, true spiritualists and healers did exist, I had personal proof! During the few months I knew him we became good friends, and he told me about his daughter, Audrey, who had died young of 'hole in the heart', which was then incurable.

I got to know Audrey quite well. Without hearing her voice, without seeing her in vision, she could, as it were, 'put' words in my head, indeed we wrote a whole book together. When she eventually left me, I could write no more, and packed it all away. You cannot believe these things unless you experience them personally. My daughter said, 'Mum, you used to be so quiet!' My husband said, 'What are you hiding from me?' Yes, a change in me could be seen by others, a second healer had given me a second kick-start.

On television, and in newspapers, we see or read about all that is evil in our society. But there is the other side, there are many who are healers walking among us. Some do not even know they are healers. They are perhaps ordinary people, not necessarily church goers or members of the Salvation Army.

In our total ignorance we say there is a 'God', and that this 'God' is 'Love', but having said that we study how to win a war, or make a quick buck.

The love we give our partner, the love we give our friends, the love we give our children, the love we give our pets – without all this what a sad world it would be.

The joy of having grandchildren.

At the time when my mother was collecting the rents, she told us that one old man who had always repeated, 'when yer dead yer done for', at last lay dying in bed. She went up to see him and said, 'Now, how about, when you are dead you are done for?' He replied, 'I be not so sure.' I would love to know what made him change his mind! Circumstances in my life make me 'not so sure'.

On the news this morning I heard that young girls were now forming gangs like the boys, wielding knives, and in some cases, guns. I know this is only a section of our society, but a section we could well do without. I wonder if any of them have ever petted a horse and have it whiffle its nose over their face, picked up a baby and rocked it till it stopped crying, ever taken a cup of tea to a hard-working mother, or helped the old lady next door across a busy road.

Chapter 5

LOOKING BACK

A good author has a beginning, middle and end to a story. When one is writing one's own biography this is not quite possible. A biography should be truth, not prediction. I may think this or that may happen, then die tomorrow.

Apart from arthritic aches and pains I enjoy my old age. I am now the child and my family look after me. My flat overlooks the Solent. Across the water I see the lights come on all along the shore of the Isle of Wight, and to the left in Gosport, and to the right in Southampton. Sometimes the sun sets in glorious colour over the water, sometimes the waves are too tiny to cause hardly a ripple, sometimes so large they seem threatening and angry. Lee on the Solent is OAP friendly. I should know because I have a mobility scooter and the Council have made many safe road crossings in the town. I wish they would add to this happy, caring, thoughtful action by making some of the Daedalus land into a country park. When 'windy Lee' has her cold wind blowing off the sea, mobility scooters could use this park, more sheltered from the wind. Gosport can live up to her claim to be 'God's Port'.

Now, though I look after myself without any hired help, I still have plenty of time to meditate on my past, so the ending of this book is not the final chapter, but the present day in which I stay poised to face the future.

I am now able to forgive my mother. She had to cope with her husband's sudden death, bringing up two children as a single parent, deal with many tenants and rent collecting, and in general get used to a totally different style of life.

Only now can I fully appreciate my sister. She was the beauty of the family, but made nothing of it, even when she won a beauty prize at Butlins. For a long time we rented a flat together, and played endless games of contract bridge with the couples living around us. The husbands were airmen who operated the huge bombers from the airfields all around Lincoln. From our flat window we could watch them fly past low down and scary. We were known as 'the girls'. We looked after their children when they had a night out, shared meals, and often settled their quarrels. My sister was more sedate, and 'grown up' than me. I tended to break my ribs falling off horses, she was not interested in any form of sport. When I did come a crash she looked after me. Our mother could throw a tennis ball in the air to serve, and then be incapable of hitting it. My sister must have inherited this!

She was a very caring person. Having taken on the duty of looking after our mother, she nursed her through a slow death of throat cancer. This entailed feeding our mother through a tube into the stomach, rushing home from a full-time office job to do it.

After my marriage my sister and I remained friendly with Tom and his wife. When he was on his own after his wife died he began to rely on my sister, now on her own, for company. She retired at sixty, and married him. She was a good wife, managed all his farm accounts, drove him around, and helped buy stock. She controlled his diabetes and kept him alive into his nineties.

The sale of Tom's farm on his death made my sister a wealthy woman but she banked it all and never changed her life style. She willed it all to me and my family. She would never leave Lincoln, although Walter and I did our best to get her to move down south to be near us.

My mother's sister, Lily, Auntie Lolla, was another person who helped make my childhood a happy one. She always invited us for Christmas. Every day pheasant, duck, turkey or goose were cooked on the large kitchen range, this delectable poultry being presents from clients who were farmers. She had married Walter Gadd, Lincoln's top man in the world of horses. Their home, off Lincoln High Street, had stables, pig sties, barns, chicken enclosures, large gardens, and even a tennis court. All this has long gone. They had one son, the only cousin I knew. Walter Gadd supplied white horses for weddings, black horses for funerals, a dray horse to pull the prison van, and various hunters to suit all sizes of rider. There were also pony traps, and carriages that were the taxis of the day. I had many a ride in these.

Walter Gadd only had to rattle the whip in its holder to make the horses bound forward faster. He took people hunting and always rode the horse that needed schooling. When Lincoln races were on, as they were in those days, he dolled himself up, immaculate in riding clothes, and on a beautifully groomed horse rode the whole length of the race course to see if all was safe. He was a small wiry man who looked his best on a horse.

Auntie Lolla always went shopping with my mother on Fridays (this was before my mother became addicted to drink). Then came another terrible blow. She died suddenly of an appendix her doctor failed to diagnose as needing removal. When it burst she was rushed to hospital, but too late, the septic fluids killed her. I remember my mother's white face when she came home from the hospital. No more holidays together at Skegness, no more joint Christmases, no more dear Auntie Lolla. After a while Walter Gadd wanted to marry my mother, but she had refused others, and preferred to remain single. I think the real reason was that in those days it was not so easy to prevent childbirth.

Auntie Lolla loved cats and could see the ones that had died still walking round the kitchen table. She had a favourite hunter. When she became pregnant this horse became jealous, and went to bite her. Walter Gadd eventually married again and had another son. He retired to a smaller place and still kept a few horses to hire out for country rides. He also stabled a racehorse reject called Bonton for its owner living nearby. I often rode Bonton to exercise her. She was highly strung and sort of bounced till she settled down and gave you a smooth, streamlined gallop along the grass verges. I wanted to buy a horse of my own, and Walter Gadd offered to help me to find one suitable. He took me to see 'Flame', a lovely gold-coloured lady's hunter. Up I got and felt him tense his muscles, and saw his ears turn back as if he were saying, 'Who the hell are you'. However I kicked his sides, and got a feel of his mouth with the reins. I felt I was on a coiled spring, and feared what tricks he had in store. Much to Walter Gadd's surprise, I said 'no' to this beautiful, sound horse, going at a reasonable price. A few days later I was at the stables to hire a ride. Walter Gadd, with very serious face said, 'I very nearly got you killed. A young girl bought Flame, and on her first ride he killed her by jumping out onto a busy road.' I said, 'I felt I would not be able to control him, he was like a coiled spring, ready to uncoil.' I always craved to buy an ex London police horse, but it was not to be. When I married, riding, tennis and hockey became a thing of the past.

Even when I married, and came to the middle chapters of my life story, I was still immature in many ways. Sometimes I compare myself with my daughter and come second best. She lives by the book, I live hit and miss.

Walter's sister and two nieces came to visit us. We sent this photo for them to hold up on the platform so we could find them quickly.

Now my book reaches its last few words. As I now sit in front of the computer facing 'Word', I still feel immature, that I have still something to learn before I die. I feel it in the air, I am ready.

With two friends in their garden. If I were to give this picture a title it would be, 'Strawberries and Cream'.

What follows is my epilogue.

Aspects of Love

Love of animals, birds etc.
Comforting, protecting, good company.

Parental love
*Heart-warming, deeply felt, protective,
very hands-on, beautiful.*

Friendly love
The enjoyment of company.

Sexual love
*The bonding of man and woman.
Humanity's greatest wonder and most powerful force.*

Spiritual love
*The most precious of all being the essence of creation itself,
the 'Word' before the physical.*

I Come to Some Conclusions

Hip operation King Edward II Hospital at Midhurst.

STUDY 1

PSALM 84

Whoever wrote Psalm 84 had the passion and conviction of a lover. Look at this:

'My soul longeth, yea, even fainteth for the courts of the Lord, my heart and my flesh crieth out for the living God.'

In fact, if you want to compose a good love letter, study the Bible! It's full of love – a love that *'goes from strength to strength'* that *'withholds no good thing'* that *'returns blessing for trust'*. Yes, that's all in Psalm 84! How can some people think the Bible dull? Love dull?

Psalm 84: *'A day in Thy courts is better than a thousand'* *'I had rather be a doorkeeper in the house of my God than dwell in the tents of wickedness.'*

What would I do with a day in the courts of God? Why not a thousand days elsewhere? What IS length – time? Their

CONTENTS are what matter. The wand of Grace may touch once, that once will give the whole 'raison d'être' of a life.

CHRISTIANITY IS A RELIGION BASED UPON THE DEPENDENCE OF MAN UPON GOD.

If you think man can go it alone, you cannot be a Christian. Is it a sign of weakness to depend or rely on God? NO! WHY? God is love, cosmic, creative love, in the highest sense of the word. To be ruled by love is strengthening, not weakening.

CHRISTIANS SAY   *'Jesus is my salvation'*
MUSLIMS SAY   *'Be your own salvation'*

Can these two convictions be reconciled?

YES, because as soon as we accept Jesus into our heart He becomes part of us, working in us and with us to fight any sin that is in us. So with Jesus within, we can be our own salvation.

A BEAUTIFUL POEM

(in translation) by Milarepa
(Here is just one verse)

*In fear of hunger I sought food, and my food is the
    meditation upon truth.
Now I fear not hunger*

THE CHILD AND THE ADULT

Mankind is a child in the Old Testament, in the New he is adult. The '*Thou shall nots*' were given to Moses to distribute when men were as children. Jesus treated men as adult, the '*Thou shall nots*' became '*Thou shall*' – love, heal, feed, teach – taboos are for children, as they grow adult they can cross the busy road, weave their steps round the lethal car to reach the other side safely. The Old Testament is full of '*Don'ts*' the New is full of '*Dos*', yet the New is born of the Old, for the '*Thou shall not kill*' of the Old becomes '*Thou shall not kill love*', or, in other words, becomes the command '*Love*'.

EVOLUTION TAKES TIME

Let us visualise a time when man will evolve many appetising protein foods from purely vegetable matter. Children never fed flesh won't desire flesh, and animal slaughter will be a thing of the past. This vegetarian way of eating, provided it is carefully planned by experts in nutrition, could eliminate some diseases, improve world health. Animal life, too, will have to follow suit, live as vegetarians or perish. 'Pest' insects, too, will have no place, their elimination is certain. As man more and more controls nature, all 'wild life' will be subject to him – the preying of beast on beast will cease, and the 'lion' really will lie down with the 'lamb'.

It is assumed that this eating of each other is necessary for the ecology of the planet – but if man is in perfect correct control, he himself can keep a balance among all life that is fit to survive. It is possible to foresee this – mankind will gain great know-how in breeding and birth control, not only for human but for animal life. Plant propagation, too, will be his care. Think of spaced-out towns, vast parklands – freedom to roam unmolested – all these things are possible – man will be ecologist supreme in the human, animal and plant kingdoms.

If all this preying of life upon life is stopped, many beautiful insects, birds and animals will be lost to us.

All this will take many, many years. Man still preys on man, let alone on beast! Many mistakes will happen to foul the project.

Evolution takes time. Vast numbers of living things perish in its relentless march – mistakes are often the sad prelude to successes – yet we must sweep our vision right forward to pierce the clouds that dim the future – one man will reach the moon, before many follow – when the world is pruned and cleaned up, man will have time and space in which to concentrate on ideas, plans and spiritual matters – he will grow in spiritual stature. Spiritual Man will be the next Age of Man, and it will be a natural evolution, following biological evolution in natural sequence.

Let's look at history – man survives from colossal wastage, suffering, and destruction – pulls himself from the very brink of self-annihilation – rushes in self-disgust from his abominations to look for better things – searches the very stars for he knows not what, only that he is dissatisfied with things as they are.

Where does God come into all this? I wonder. Evolution does not make nonsense out of God, it makes more sense – it is God's method. And Jesus? God in focus for me to see – if man were his own god he would have perished long ago. Divine intervention, spiritual leadership are realities. Technology takes man so far, but still leaves him unsatisfied. A child plays happily with his toys, but when he is older he searches for happiness of spirit – the sort of happiness that needs no props, but is within, as a rock of strength.

Because we are a long, long way from where we should be, and because sins and evils scream with scarlet voice, and tempt with instant 'kicks' and 'seem' to be the only way to 'get anywhere' we lost heart and often kill the very ones who would save us.

Tree house South Africa.

PERFECT HEAVEN

It is difficult to visualise total good, life without dark – the perfect heaven. We are very, very far away, but the Kingdom of God does exist as pure light, as pure love, not needing darkness, not needing hate to give it existence or backdrop. Health is a state of being, not needing sickness to give it reality. Why should we need a backcloth of suffering and ugliness to make us appreciate the grace and the glory of absolute perfection? How wrong they are who think life would be dead dull without the kicks of sin! Limitless joy, in limitless variety of expression! Can love be boring? Colour, richness, beauty, music... are these dull? We must all set our sights higher, to say fatalistically there must be evil, is evil itself speaking. At present there's a kind of drugged apathy – freedom that isn't really freedom but ungodly licence – shades of evil – thieving, lusting, warring – as Isaiah said, we have unclean lips, and dwell in a world of unclean lips.

The perfect heaven is not yet reached by the human race, not by a long, long way – but some 'see through a glass darkly' some have 'intimations of immortality', some, though they 'stain the white radiance of eternity', are touched by a joy 'out-of-this-world'. At present there is no starry-eyed world of love – and – no– kill, when love itself is being killed bombed, blasted tortured, twisted, out of existence. The melting pot of life won't be gentle. It is an inexorable discipline – very often the two-edged sword must cut away bloodily to cleanse.

THE ART GALLERY

We wandered round the art gallery, just as one might listen to music played as background to other things, or half notice the flowers and shrubs in a friend's garden. However, some paintings could not be ignored.

One, directly in front, level with the eyes, was called 'The Message'. It was a study of hands, and in it one could find a blessing, a curse, a confession, a healing, a supplication, a refusing, a denial, a prayer, a hating – according to the degree of concentration given by the onlooker.

Another was called 'The Journey'. A young man and woman, holding hands, seemed to walk right out of the picture to meet us. What would be the journey of their life, how would it impinge on mine in reality, in imagination?

There was a bold, Salvador Dali like creation. This was called 'The Crucifixion'. There was a blaze of fire, the ash of destruction, and a white promise of peace – Nuclear war? The awesome uplifting of man through the agony of man's own follies? I visualised not one death, but thousands, not one agony, but every pain in the body and mind of man. I felt within myself the tremendous impact of God's braking power, the twisting of the scorpion's tail into its own body.

I needed reassurance, consolation – I looked round – I feasted my eyes on a riot of beautifully blended colours – 'The

Country Garden', and this picture was as calm as water after tsunami.

TABLE TENNIS

Plan your manoeuvres. Keep your opponent on the run from corner to corner, volleying back and forehand drives to right and left. Drive your opponent right back, then drop the ball gently, just over the net, out of reach or to bounce at an irretrievable angle – or of course smash hit that's a sure winner!

THOSE OLD BLOCKBUSTERS
'WHAT IS REAL?' – 'WHAT IS TRUTH?'

Speaking as a human on planet Earth, with all my limitations as such, I would class anything as 'real' as my family, as 'real' as all that I could touch, see, and smell. Some would query, 'Is the Bible true?' – 'Is Jesus just a myth, a built-up legend?' Yet it is a fact that the Bible and Jesus are as 'alive' and 'real' in today's world as ever they were. The spiritual leaders, the healers, the ones who 'Hunger and thirst after righteousness' the ones who don't pass by, but stop, not to stare, but to offer all the help they can – what gives these people their 'Hearts of Gold?' Often the Grace and Truth that beautifies them can be felt, seen and touched in the mind and by the body of those fortunate enough to be in contact. One can say, 'Reality' is 'Truth' – and 'Truth' is 'Reality'.

FAITH AND RELIGIONS

Faith and religions cause a lot of trouble. Growing babies cause a lot of trouble! Are we to say, 'No more babies'? Established Church is the library that holds the precious volumes of spiritual thought. People have tried living without 'Religion' – what have they achieved? A bomb may rid the world of some evil people, or end a particular war, but it won't rid the world of the evil that causes war. Evil is a 'force' only to be destroyed by a superior 'force' of spiritual origin. What will cure Man's great depression best? Drugs? Or the grace to master it himself? Every person born is important – he needs personal revelation, personal responsibility, the individual right to discover truth – the great cathedral is built of many stones, the strength and shape of each individual stone matter, its placing, its relation to the whole.

WHY DO I LOVE GRACE DARLING?

I read her biography, by Eva Hope, some thirty-five years ago. A lot of this book is Victorian sentimentalism and moralising, and probably does not stick to fact, but it is lovingly, and at times, poetically, written – and I 'fell in love'. I felt that Eva Hope loved her subject, in fact she was 'misty-eyed' – and the love came over to me. Later I found another biography, by Richard Armstrong – this, no doubt, is more strictly correct factually, but reads as dry as a dead hornet, pulls poor old Eva Hope apart, makes mincemeat of her love, and goes to great lengths to prove Grace both simple and facially deformed. However, I did find in this book the one and only picture of Grace that speaks with truth – it is a sketch by Perlee Parker. I tore it out, and kept it by me – my ideal woman! It is just one more paradox, that places this lovely portrait in a book that denies beauty to Grace Darling.

What a great source of love lies embedded in literature, art, and music! A source we can all tap – nothing snowballs like love, and its first spark can glow in a written word. What did that old man, St. Paul, write to his Churches? *'Beloved, let us love one another, let us greet one another with an Holy kiss.'* Now isn't that something!

Bread Ukrainian style.

IN MY MIND'S EYE, AND
THE MUSTARD SEED

In my mind's eye I still see the starved Biafran babies –
darling, curly haired, brown skinned, plump cuddly bundles,
reduced to skeletal wrecks of misery, deformed specks of
human flotsam. I see the nuclear bomb scarred Japanese, still
living witness to the wretched result of the abominable hatred
between peoples. I now see the wild faced, bomb throwing,
gun pointing, terrorists and high-jackers, the final result of
society's evils – throw-ups from a frothing scum of discontent,
gone berserk. I saw the drug-crazed 'Hippies', now I see the
'opt-outs', mental homes full of psychological 'cases' – men
and women, children even, pressurised to insanity by tensions
and evils spreading like rot over mankind. I saw the babies
born deformed by drug-taking mothers, now I see the babies
born as unwanted by-products of animal lust, or murdered by
abortion.

Yes, in my mind I can scan a rapid panorama of the world – I can see every cruelty, every neglect, every murder in the heart. There's slaughter and infliction of suffering to make the mind boggle, of a scale to make the body faint at the problem of tackling such a vast mountain of evil. Nothing escapes, neither home, school, church, government.

One man can destroy or pollute a nation – one woman can denigrate womanhood – the very power of evil is its persistent strength – its cunning ability to hide itself to camouflage itself so that the innocent are fooled – this alone – this ability to be there and not be recognised – a whole nation can seem to be OK, but hidden inside is a cancer of the devil. Cancers hurt, cancers destroy, only the cancer wins.

Well, for those who deplore this state of affairs, and there are many, we have the mustard seed to scatter in the mess. TV programmes like *This is Your Life*, or *Hearts of Gold* or *Surprise, Surprise* spotlight the other side of the coin – spotlight the sowers of the mustard seeds of care, of love, of compassion, of wholesome living.

Mustard seeds are small, but they produce a bold, tangy leaf, not to be ignored – many, many seeds, many, many seeds of bold, tangy sheer goodness, scattered by many, many who take pity, who care, who risk all to help the afflicted – these people give us hope – a mustard seed of hope.

Son Julian at Greenwich.

TALES THAT RING TRUE

Let's take a random sample of Bible stories – they ring true because they are taken from life, not fancy or make-believe – what about the little man who couldn't see over the heads of the crowd, so he climbed a tree to catch a glimpse of Jesus passing by – '*Today I dine with you,*' said Jesus, noticing him, and rewarding his effort – that obviously happened. Then there is that amazing story of the sick man who was crash lowered through a roof, bed and all, by his relatives and friends, so that he could be placed at Jesus' feet – lowered through the roof, because that was the only way he could be brought close enough to Jesus for healing in that crowded room. Somebody obviously witnessed this and recalled it with gusto to the gospel writers – second or third hand – yes – 2,000 years old – this tale rings true. If I were bedridden like that man, I would like my friends to make such a stupendous effort on my behalf.

What about the Bible women – all of them, perhaps briefly mentioned, stand out, real people caught and 'snapped' in a living moment of their lives.

Jesus' own mother, worried about her pregnancy, did, we are told, the most natural things in the world, went to consult her relation – Elizabeth – went for comfort and advice. Can we doubt this?

Perhaps the most vivid story tells of the woman who wept over Jesus' feet, washing them with the tears of repentance then wiping them dry with her hair. Finally anointing His head with a precious ointment. *'She's a sinner!'* cry the horrified assembly. *'And she wastes good ointment!'* *'Her sins, which are many, are forgiven, for she loves much,'* was Jesus' answer. Could this unique story be a figment of the writer's imagination?

One can actually picture the woman of Samaria, at the well, who after talking to Jesus there, went home and spread abroad – *'Come see a man who told me all things whatever I did.'*

We can also picture the woman who touched the hem of Jesus' garment, seeking healing – so humble, so very trusting.

Perhaps the icing on the cake is composed of the sisters Martha and Marty – one cannot deny their existence! Martha, the busy one, always cumbered about with the chores, and getting impatient with Mary, content to sit at Jesus' feet and listen. *'Lord, bid Mary come and help me!'* cried poor Martha, but Jesus, though he loved both equally, protected Mary, saying *'she hath chosen that good part that shall not be taken away.'* This is no fairy tale, it is right down-to-earth – these two women are with us today, the 'doer' and the 'thinker' and both, as Jesus recognised, need their space in a balanced society. It was their brother, Lazarus, over whose body Jesus cried, before bringing him back to life – and it is these homely scenes that 'humanise' Jesus.

FIRST IMPRESSIONS AND THIRD THOUGHTS

Let us suppose a Mr D meets a Miss E, and they 'click' or 'hit it off' at once. Miss E thinks Mr D the answer to a maiden's prayer. Later she learns that he is divorced, that he supports a bastard child, that he has been in prison. She 'ditches' him promptly. The sad thing is this, perhaps he was right for Miss E, just her man, and she 'instinctively' knew this on first meeting – that first impression was giving her the all-clear. For her alone he could have become all she thought him to be – the full man, the perfect husband for her. Later she marries, safely, in accordance with her parents' wishes, a sedate and respectable business man of impeccable character. She finds herself bored and unhappy, and becomes neurotic – and only she has an inkling as to why. Mr D, being 'ditched' by the one woman capable of understanding him and loving him, goes downhill, and amply justifies the tittle-tattle of the gossips.

Perhaps Mr D had married a pretty but worthless baggage, and the divorce, though deplorable, was not his fault. Perhaps he supports the bastard child out of the goodness of his nature, maybe he could have got out of it easily. Perhaps he landed in prison because he robbed Peter to pay Paul, Robin Hood style, again deplorable, but hardly an awesome crime. Perhaps Mr D is a bit dented by the follies of his youth – but he did love Miss E and she knew it – he gave her alone a special love which is a very precious commodity – it can burn a sordid past up and use the ashes to fertilise a new future. Miss E inspired such a love, and she shouldn't have third thoughts to combat the second thoughts and justify the first thoughts!

WE CAN DO IT!

I wonder what the returning warriors expected to find when the homing troop ships grumbled their weary way to Portland. Certainly a brave new world glittering with gadgets to make life easier for the common man – this was emerging – and the Duke in his castle was becoming redundant, or, at least, a peep show. World War II had thrown its nuclear bomb. The Nazi witches had danced their war dance round the cauldron of Europe till they had evoked an evil genie strong enough to turn on its maker. This genie rose in blazing mushroom puff from his shattered bottle, searing and despoiling everything in his orbit – out-sinning sin, a ghastly ghoul, a horror more horrible than any horror known to man. The witches, the war mongers, brought to heel at last by this super-killer of their own evocation, hoisted the white flag. The witch dance ended abruptly, but the genie, thus released, lies on, back in his bottle, it is true, yet lurking there, waiting for one more chance – he will jump at it, and this time really show his strength, his demon strength, to destroy utterly this foolish world, and free himself forever in his demon kingdom. The genie chuckles and grows fat. He flexes his muscles, rattles his chains, bides his time. Soon, very soon, he will be strong enough to shatter his confining walls, and offer his services to those who hate, lust, envy and kill. He is dynamic, he is noisy, he screams with a scarlet voice.

The time will come – the stop – the think – when man will cease his greedy grub-like activities, enter the pupa state of metamorphosis, and concentrate all his energy on winning his wings. Man lingers in and enjoys his present state because he revels in the great laws that compel him to eat, sleep, and reproduce. He clings to this state, fearing to lose his perks, failing to realise that, 'with wings', he loses nothing – he gains much. Everything is there, gloriously there, more there. Tremendous life energies 'work' in apparent calm – this is deceptive. Activity within the cell, most especially the nerve cell, is undercover work, potent yet silent – in this lies man's future. By the development of the human nerve cell spiritual evolution will follow biological evolution in natural sequence. Throughout evolution there is a life force which is 'true' and which will eventually shed everything but 'truth'. In man's first step is implicated the last, and all that goes between. Should he cry, 'halt, enough!' he would kill his very soul.

Man is strong, he has a starter to truth, and is thus connected to whole truth, and may dip into its vast reserves. Just as man has fouled and overcrowded his cage, so he can clean it up. As man steps forward step by step, he will see the next step, and realise it is possible to reach it. In the crowded cage, there are those, even now, who will put a hand out, a foot out, break out altogether – then – who knows – we cannot know till it is done – it must be done. Step by step, like the mountaineer, the last foothold to the top will be forged by the man, forged for the job. The vista will be seen by him, we can only guess at it now. There is no going back to the 'simple life' – man's very nature is to advance. In all man's strivings, inspite of all his dreadful mistakes, there is this urge to know all, and in the knowing – live – live in the true peace and order of the conqueror – a man of knowledge and strength. The 'Whole-Soul' of mankind – that's what matters – that's what has a future – unless we strive for this, individual lives are meaningless. We can but hope the fires man kindles are for his own cleansing – that the bloody pruning knife in his hand may make room for blooms of quality. There's a lot to be done, the task seems impossible – but what a task – what reward!

(modern Ukraine still has some picturesque scenes)

It is a task fit for a man – he already has the equipment and the clues. Though many, many, will fall out, some will come to give great boost and advancement. What energy is released when fears are removed! What a spur to activity is given when reward is in sight! As evil snowballs, so good gathers its own fascinating momentum. The massed populations of nations compressed upon a world from which they cannot escape in bulk, do compromise the nerve-cell factory of new thinking – spiritual man – yes spiritual man.

(Please note – when, in this writing, the word 'man' is used, it is a shortening for 'mankind' i.e. both male and female. In the same way, we call God, 'He' Jesus, 'He' surely the Holy Ghost is Grace the 'She'.)

One can overleap mighty catastrophes, such as nuclear destruction, mass suicides of many kinds – to see the emergence of the end product – thinking man. There was a first cell, protoplasm, an amoeba, there will be Spiritual Man. He will emerge, not by magic, or sudden miracle, but by the slow process of normal evolution, the development of the nerve-cell. There are, thank God, many 'Souls' whose 'Acts' follow their 'conversions' – many more who speak God's words without necessarily knowing their source. In this world where we are given a span of physical life 'Many are called but few are chosen' and these 'few' these very few, take us forward, a few have the visions, a few manage the 'acts'.

Let us imagine the beauty of the end product, use all our energy to sustain this beauty – feel fully stretched, giving all – lose oneself in the wonders – fly as a bird over the edge of the world to hear the Angels sing – the Angels which are the seed of man, implanted for his flowering.

MY FRIEND C.S. LEWIS

C.S. Lewis, his use of words so exact, his English so perfect, and after conversion to Christianity so sincere, he wins a friend he knows nothing about, sure, he is my friend!

This intellectual, this Oxford Don, clean living and proudly agnostic, suddenly takes to Christianity like a duck to water. Having become a Christian, and being the person he is, he probes and studies WHY – What made ME a Christian? Is it reasonable to be a Christian? What should I do about it?

For starters he wrote many books re. all this. Put in a nutshell, his answer to 'what made me a Christian?' is JOY – a joy found IN this world, yet coming from OUTSIDE this world – the beauty and mystery of the music of Wagner and the outstanding scenarios of untouched nature were some of the channels for this JOY. The joy mentioned in John 15 – Jesus to his disciples – *'ask, and ye shall receive, that your JOY may be full'*. The answer to 'Is it reasonable to be a Christian?' is YES. The true Christians (not necessarily church-goers) are reasonable because they comprehend the raison d'être of life. The answer to 'What should I do about it?' is – 'I will write of my faith, use my gifts, to spread Christianity.'

He does just that. It is a sign of the truly converted that they are PUSHED by the Grace of conversion to spread the Gospel – for Grace is too big to hold – it HAS to be handed on – if that cannot be done the frustration and unhappiness are hard to bear – like being full of love and no one to love! C.S. Lewis often tries to explain things that might 'put one off' the Bible – such as – Are miracles possible? Or Is Jesus one big fake? Miracles, he says, are more than possible! They are life itself – life being one big miracle – one big unexplainable! Jesus a fake? How come He is 'alive and kicking' so to speak, and has called me? The Virgin birth? Isn't all birth of God, or the Spirit of God? Raising the dead? God can and does rearrange matter continuously. C.S. Lewis plunges in head first, it's a tonic to read. The Bible and Jesus are swallowed whole – and what a good thing! There's no sifting, no screening, no purges, all that was written all those years ago is absorbed into him – whether there are historical inaccuracies, ecstatically loving exaggerations – too many 'begats'! mysteries, miracles, or indeed any other floss and flotsam that cynics toss to and fro. In this pot-pourri C.S. Lewis finds his JOY, finds the BREAD that feeds him, finds his life's purpose, finds the PEACE that is not of this world. He also finds FUN in all this – *'It's fun, it's like being in a club'* he writes – The Grace Club. There are some who never get into the rich experience of the Grace Club, they neither believe nor know it's there. It's difficult to fathom why some are left out – Jesus had this cryptic thing to say. *'Many are called, but few are chosen'.* Also, *'In my Father's house are many mansions'.*

One cannot add to those pronouncements of Jesus, one can only accept them. the 'eat, sleep, and be merry' brigade, who often live in the gutter of life, may, when adverse circumstances crop up, find that eating won't console – in fact one 'goes off' it, that sleeping won't console – in fact one 'goes off' that too – and as for being merry? The Grace Club offers the consolation that's needed – a mystic food of which there is no limit, a cosmic love that is also individual, a joy that transcends merriment.

C.S. Lewis found that The Grace Club captured him, not the other way round – for Grace spreads like germs, highly contagious and unseen.

'May the hand of God rest over my son.' A father sees his son take ship to America during the famine in Ireland.

THE CHRISTMAS CACTUS

Right in Mid-Winter, on the very tip of each leaf form, that hang, candelabra-like, a flower bud appears. Then a curious thing – these buds wait and wait and wait, just like that, until they feel a few days of warmth, then – wham – they grow and open into bloom. It's quite a lesson in how to know the right moment!

GOOD HEAVENS, WE'RE NOT SOLID AT ALL

What have physicists discovered? That all 'Matter' is a 'Wave' and an unpredictable 'Quanta' of energy – there is no 'solid' ultimate substance. The Cosmos is a 'Whole' made of 'Energy waves' that (to us) make 'Forms'. 'We' are a part of that 'Whole' and the 'Whole' is a 'Wave'. What does a wave suggest? Movement – force – energy – rhythm – tempo, fast/slow – penetration – continuity – variation. One could say this adds up to something interesting, elusive, indeterminate, flexible – something that has the potential to evolve, change, develop. What a whole vast history lies in front of us, the human race, just because of this fluidity.

THE SUBTLE AND THE OBVIOUS

We whirl around in Cosmic space, and yet we seem so still –
It's obvious we're this and that – and haven't we free-will?
It's obvious I'm here and now – I touch, I see, I hear!
O, subtle God, come hold me dear – I faint, I fear, this
*   awesome obviousness.*

THE PROMISE OF THE APRICOT ROSE

I'll take you back to Minstead, and Furzey's fragrant bower,
Within my secret, scented heart you'll find your perfect hour.
I'll take you back to sea-lashed Farne, and Longstone's
*   guiding light.*
Within my silken petals curled, you'll taste a love as bright.
I'll take you back to Chalice Well, and Glastonbury's peace.
Within the Sapphire loving-cup the cross of death shall cease.

TIBETAN POEM – BE CONTENT

My son, as monastery be content with the body
For the bodily substance is the palace of divinity.
As a teacher be content with the mind
For knowledge of the truth is the beginning of holiness
As a book be content with outward things, for their number is a
*   symbol of the way of deliverance.*

Yes! The Ukraine again – digging potatoes for dinner.

MATURITY

Golden harvest of maturity,
*   come feed the wholesome leavened bread*
*   from your rich cornfield gathered.*

Golden harvest of a life,
*   come give with zest the brimming cup of crimson wine*
*   from out your vineyard pressed.*

Golden harvest of a soul,
*   come shed on me the coloured leaves*
*   from these few precious Autumn years conceived.*

HAPPINESS IS

The being alone – yet not lonely
The being two, yet not two – one!

RON'S THOUGHTS

Almost fifty years together.

PEACE

'My peace I give unto you, my peace I leave with you, not as the world giveth give I unto you' Jesus.

Peace and Grace go hand in hand – they are the very root, stem and flower of blossoming humanity.

In our world Peace and Grace may come to an individual or a group, or even a multitude, to give rebirth, regeneration, and sanctity, and it may come suddenly or slowly, and at any age. This peace is the direct manifestation of God's Grace, just like the Grace and Truth instantly seen in Jesus... Roget's Thesaurus defines Grace as 'gift' 'beauty' 'mercy' amongst other things.

A sort of peace in our world may be brought about by the actual physical taking up of arms and fighting evils such as slavery, oppression, poverty. 'Yamamah' as they say in Saudi Arabia. – 'Dove of peace'. These Yamamah treaties, the Dove of peace treaties the Saudis make with Great Britain to buy weapons of war, mainly Tornado Fighters and battle tanks, are 'To keep the peace' 'To frighten enemies off' so they say.

This 'Yamamah' peace or safety relies on the holding of deadly weapons, in large quantities (more than the perceived enemy) 'Star War project' in the U.S.A. is the same (even worse!).

This type of peace will never hold, will never benefit humanity, as would the peace won by Grace.

Will Jesus eventually do battle with Satan, real blood and thunder? NO.

Jesus, not as the world giveth, but as He giveth, will bring the world to peace.

'Whenever I've been to Bournemouth you couldn't stick a pin between bodies on the beach, picnic parties in the gardens, and cars on the roads,' I stated flatly.

'Ah,' replied John, 'you have to live there, with luck!'

'You mean, it isn't always high season,' I said.

'Exactly,' answered John, 'but remember, it's these very crowds that sustain Bournemouth. Because of them and the trade they bring, her gardens blossom and her concert halls ring, and there is money to clean and replenish her sands.'

'But cars, students, and layabouts just about take over!' I said, still sceptical.

'Not for long,' John persisted, 'and people cope.'

'I suppose they do,' I gave in, and John went on, 'Anyway, there's a fundamental quality about Poole Bay that nothing can destroy – already it's survived years of exploitation – and who are we to deny anyone a taste of its cream! Why, the sea itself dominates – rules – who can disobey? It holds sway over weather and people, both have to mould themselves to its moods. Yet this great sea gentles itself into the beautiful sweep of bay, with its sand and natural cliff stretching from Sandbanks to Hengistbury Head – gently creams in – and remains for every last toddler to try his first cautious dabble.'

'Surely there are storms too!' I expostulated.

'Oh yes, a magnificent adult spectacle – a self-cleaning – a purification of the much used sand!'

'Bournemouth draws people like a magnet – they either spend their fortunes there, or make their fortunes there. The old live out their days soaking up the sun, while the young and energetic raise their gaudy hotels and flatlet houses ever

higher and higher, making ever bigger and bigger webs to catch the tourist fly. As you see, the tin-god car demands more and more space, the din-god, entertainment more emporium – yet – whatever ghastly monstrosity man sets down on this lovely coast – there's something indestructible about its beauty. The receptive soul can still find inspiration there.'

THE AMERICAN EVANGELISTS

He's a tub-thumping evangelist, he's a tonic, he banishes the sceptic and the disbeliever by throwing Jesus and the Bible at them with trumpets and drums and huge banners, mass choirs, impressive preaching and demonstrations of conversion to inspire the most timid. Who is this? It is the powerfully charismatic and convinced Christian, Billy Graham.

Billy Graham is not everyone's cup of tea – but he does get results! If you cannot stand his razzmatazz, at least read his book, *The Jesus Generation* and the books of others he has inspired like *The Cross and the Switchblade* by David Wilkerson, or *Run Baby run* by Nicky Cruz.

The dynamic activity of Billy Graham in 'slum areas' of America converted some terrible characters from utter depravity to clean living. He would hold huge mass rallies in the most hostile of environments. One of his 'converts' a die-hard criminal who at one time could neither speak the 'King's English' nor write – only hate and kill – eventually wrote his own story – this was Nicky Cruz. It makes compulsive reading.

It's a fact! Billy Graham and his converts are 'full to bursting' with Jesus' love – they have to 'blow their top or die'! They DO get results, they DO reform the wicked.

One has to ask oneself the question, 'Is Billy Graham MY cup of tea?' No? well, supposing I had 'gone to the dogs', taken to drugs, committed violent crimes, landed in prison? The Billy Graham type may help me where others might fail – just because he goes at you with 'all guns firing' so to speak.

Right on the other side is the one who spreads the love of Jesus by never saying a word about it – this one LIVES it, spreads it by example, makes the onlooker crave to have it, to copy. This one's prayers may benefit an unknown multitude. This one is not a big public mass media figure.

Just as Billy Graham might be a 'God-send' to some, so the quiet Priest might be a 'God-send' to others – one is lucky if the right one happens along!

Tortures, burnings, murders and wars have been done in the name of God – we have a lot to live down – let's give anyone a hearing who has a better way.

GRACE DARLING'S GARDEN

My father's grave in Belgium.

In brash, sprawling, modern Southampton – there it is – many pass it without so much as a glance, as they rush from car park or docks to the main shopping area. I am no exception, but this particular day I struck lucky. Painted clockwork men in a bell tower performed their little act of striking the hour, just as I was passing, and I looked up, intrigued. It was a church, surely, but a bombed-out ruin of a church. Then I noticed bushes, and a haze of blue flowers in what should have been the nave. I crossed the road to have a peep, indeed, a closer look. The one-time nave had been transformed by some inspired, and unknown-to-me gardener into a charming and peaceful mini-garden. An old man was sat on a seat, reading a newspaper and sunning himself contentedly. A woman with a pram, and holding an open magazine, gazed into space. In the far right-hand corner was set a large anchor with a plaque reading – 'This church is dedicated to seamen'.

A young girl ran into the garden, and rested herself against the anchor. Her hair glinted in the sun, and wispy fronds waved and curled round her face. Perhaps this girl was nothing like the Grace Darling of Longstone Lighthouse fame, whose name adorns many a lifeboat, and has done so over some hundred years. Yet the poise of this young girl of today, the natural waving of her hair, brought this national heroine of long ago vividly to mind.

I always think of this place as Grace Darling's garden – I wonder if it is still there! Time marches on, places change. I went to the library, and read up all there was to find. Somehow Grace Darling (what a lovely name!) has become a friend in spirit, a kind of enrichment I hold very precious.

HER SONG

This is my promise, that I will meet you, and you will know me,
*   smile a welcome*
Over the bridge of death
Soon you will greet me, and I will hold you
Over the bridge of new birth.
This is my promise, my sign is upon it, the waves round my
*   Longstone*
Lapping my Longstone
When death and birth meet.

A FEW FINAL WORDS

I feel I must come right up to date. I say a lot about the past, now the present bombards me, and points to a future full of new and exciting experiences. I started to write this autobiography about a year ago. Before I can start any writing I must have compelling inspiration from a spiritual source, over which I have no control, and which comes to me uninvited and suddenly. 'Out of the blue', we say. Some forty years ago my inspiration came from a lovely young girl called Audrey who had died some years previously, and who loved her father, the healer, using me as her contact with him. At this time I had no typewriter, nor computer. When I held pen over paper, it was if she took over my thoughts. Without sound or vision, poems, stories, even little sketches came to me. There is a lot of ME in this book, but I could not have done it without her. Unfortunately, I had to pack it all away, I had a hotel to run, three children to look after, and a husband not at all sympathetic to me 'pen pushing.' Audrey went away, and I could not get her back. Her parting 'words' were, 'Do something for Grace'. Over the years I have pondered on what she meant, and always feel I am letting her down, for WHAT have I ever done 'for Grace'. Can I make money, and give it to the Salvation Army good causes? But my writing is immature, no horror, no violence, no sexual porn. It will not sell, a silly boy/girl romance would get the market. Audrey had another parting shot. 'Get going, or you will die and your daughter inherit all there is still to do'.

This year I have been given a great push to 'Get Going' and inspiration for this autobiography came bursting upon me, again unlooked for, and suddenly, 'Out the blue'. Again it is spiritual, of the soul, but this time from a living person. I could tune into this person and take in a loving and giving spirituality that was hidden deep within. This experience was entirely new to me, I could not handle it. I blurted out words that just shot into my head, like, 'You give me a lot', and I said this many times without understanding what I was implying. I was filled with a kind of energy and joy, which eventually inspired me and gave me the energy to start writing again after all those empty years.

Looking back I can see the error of my ways, for I lost a friendship that meant so much to me. I should have kept quiet, for this man had no idea of the effect he had on me, only wanted to offer a kind of cold platonic friendship, and for some reason, shied away from any form of physical contact. I supposed I scared him off. But I can control myself and would still cry, 'never go, never leave me'. Fortunately, I have been very busy moving house, or rather, flats, and this has left me little time to grieve over lost friendships, but try to benefit from the good things they have given. I have moved into 'Sheltered Housing', where there is a good social life, and a superb Warden who is like a mother to all 60 flats in the building.

Yes, life goes on into the future, even one's last few years can be full of good surprises.